The Jonestown

The Shocking True Story of Jim Jones,
Mind Control, and Mass Tragedy

By

Cortney T. Greenstein

copyright@2025

TABLE OF CONTENT

CHAPTER ONE..................................9

The People's Temple: Our Founding Place..9

The Rise to Power of a Cult Leader: Jim Jones..15

CHAPTER TWO 21

Moving on to Guyana 21

CHAPTER THREE 29

Jonestown: The Brutal Truth 29

A Heart-breaking End for Leo Ryan.31

CHAPTER FOUR..............................38

Jonestown Tragedy 38

Lessons from Jonestown 47

END **52**

The People's Temple and Jim Jones stand out as some of the most infamous cults and mass suicides in history. The People's Temple was a once-promising religious group that championed racial integration, social justice, and equality, established by the charismatic yet manipulative Jim Jones. Over time, it evolved into a cult that was not only extremely rigid but also possibly dangerous.

For some people, the absurdity of the story can actually make it more powerful than the tragedy itself. Jones' conspiracy beliefs led nearly a thousand followers of a cult leader to retreat into seclusion in Guyana. What has caused many people to lose interest in their surroundings? How deeply were they deceived by a con artist pretending to be a preacher?

This account sheds light on the mystery of the Jonestown Massacre and provides answers to lingering questions. This book looks into the rise and fall of the People's Temple, concentrating on Jim Jones' methods for exerting control over his followers in detail. Jim Jones and his followers relocated the People's Temple to Guyana. The infamous Jonestown colony was founded by Jones, and sadly, more than 900 people lost their lives or took their own lives due to the events that transpired there. It serves as a chilling reminder of how persuasive leaders can lead their followers to unthinkingly obey their every directive.

The book highlights the lasting effects of the disaster and the insights we can gain to avoid similar tragedies down the line.

PROLOG

On November 18, 1978, around 900 members of the Peoples Temple, an American cult, lost their lives in the tragic event known as the "Jonestown Massacre." Jim Jones (1931–1978) was the leader behind this terrible event. Guyana is a country in South America that was home to the colony of Jonestown. Peoples Temple in Indiana was established by Jones during the 1950s. In the 1960s, he moved his followers to California. The captivating yet authoritarian preacher led around a thousand of his followers into the Guyanese jungle following some unfavorable media coverage in the 1970s. He truly believed that this would be the place for their perfect society. Sadly, U.S. Representative Leo Ryan was among the five people in his group who lost their lives on November 18, 1978, during a visit to Jonestown. Their trip was sparked by questions surrounding claims of mistreatment. Later that day, Jones had his followers drink a deadly punch while he and his armed bodyguards stood guard.

CHAPTER ONE

The People's Temple: Our Founding Place

After three decades of prominence in modern society, Jim Jones met a tragic downfall when he commanded his followers to take their own lives by gathering around a pot of poisoned punch. During the 1940s and 1950s, he became well-known for his humanitarian efforts and for founding a groundbreaking church in the Midwest that welcomed people of various colors and nationalities. His efforts to eliminate segregation in Indiana garnered him backing from civil rights activists. After relocating his flock from Indianapolis to California, he continued to share the same message of love. Their main goal was to help those who are less fortunate and marginalized, enabling them to partake in the successes of society. They subtly showed their backing for socialism, wishing that the public would embrace this contentious belief system.

During this period, Jim Jones started to explore faith healing. He sought to attract more supporters and funding for his cause, so he made bold assertions about miraculous occurrences, such as a cure for cancer. Instead of cancer, he skillfully showcased bits of decaying chicken, much like a magician revealing a clever illusion.

The Jonestown massacre stands out as one of the most devastating man-made disasters in American history, holding a prominent place until the tragic events of September 11 unfolded. Even during his most tragic times, Jim Jones, with his megalomaniac tendencies, didn't possess remarkable authority. Jones was born in a small town in Indiana on May 13,

1931. In the early 1950s, he started his journey as a Christian preacher in the smaller churches of Indianapolis. He appointed himself to this role. Jones, a fascinating individual, made numerous efforts to gather enough money to build his own church. Among the more unusual approaches taken in these efforts was the practice of selling live monkeys from door to door.

During the mid-1950s, Jones founded the first Peoples Temple church in Indianapolis. At that time, it was quite rare for churches in the Midwest to feature a congregation that was so racially diverse. Redwood Valley is a small community in Mendocino County, Northern California, where Jones relocated his congregation in 1965. A forward-thinking priest built a church in Los Angeles during the early 1970s and relocated the headquarters to San Francisco. In 1956, Jim Jones founded the Peoples Temple, aiming to help those in need. It is a diverse faith with a commendable mission. Jones established the Peoples Temple in Indianapolis before moving it to Redwood Valley,

California in 1966. Jones imagined a society where everyone collaborated to enhance life for everyone. He initially planned to build a complex in a different country, but he ended up starting the project in California. Due to his total authority over the secluded compound, members of the Peoples Temple would enjoy unrestricted access to the community and be shielded from interference by the US government.

The Rise to Power of a Cult Leader: Jim Jones

Jones became well-known as a significant figure in San Francisco due to his commanding presence. He gained the favor of public servants and journalists thanks to his charitable contributions, and he was able to sway voters' decisions, which impacted the outcome of the election. A free community dining hall, drug treatment programs, and legal aid were just a few of the many resources made accessible to the needy by Peoples Temple. Young, idealistic people who wished to make a change in the world were particularly drawn to Jones and his message of social equality and racial justice. People in Jones's expanding flock began talking about the man they called "Father" all the time. One expose from 1977 in New West magazine estimated that there were around 20,000 Peoples Temple followers, while other sources have given varying figures. Former members have accused the group of manipulating or pressuring them into relinquishing their homes, children, and personal possessions. Jones was accused of creating "cancer healings" and the victims described their experiences of physical assault in their statement. As a result of the unfavorable press and the overwhelming number of questions, Jones became more reserved, which manifested itself in his choice to wear dark sunglasses and travel with bodyguards. A socialist paradise he had promised his followers could be built in Guyana was finally within reach after considerable persuasion. Constantly, a great deal of bizarre stuff began to happen. It was disturbing to see that

Jones's concern for his environment was increasing. A recurring theme in his speeches was the impending nuclear Armageddon, which he said was caused by the administration's foolishness. His status in the media was beginning to shift, despite the support of notable figures such as First Lady Rosalynn Carter and California Governor Jerry Brown. Following the resignation of numerous influential members, the Peoples Temple experienced a violent and extensively documented split. In response, the group began to circulate rumors that the defectors were plotting a violent attack on the church. Over time, the church's hierarchy became more rigid. The administrative positions in the temple were filled with wealthy white ladies, even though the majority of the worshippers were African-American. Staged healings, trinket selling, and solicitation mailings were some of the complex fundraising tactics planned by the highest tiers in more covert locations. It was starting to look more and more like Jones was just interested in the religious components of his church for the sake of furthering his own agenda. He considered the positive impact he may have on society with the unwavering support of his dedicated fan base. As he boldly pursued his social ambitions, violent leftist organizations and Marxist authorities took note of his extreme ideology. After the transition and the influx of defectors, the media did not hesitate to center their attention on the cult. As a result, Jones sent out rescue teams and a private plane to retrieve the people who managed to stay alive.

CHAPTER TWO

Moving on to Guyana

Jones found the ideal level of solitude in the South American republic of Guyana, where he eventually made his home. In 1973, he started leasing land from the government of Guyana and brought in loggers to cut down trees. The Jonestown Agricultural Settlement was unable to advance in its development due to the inconvenience of transporting construction materials to the location. At the start of 1977, while Jones was still in the US, there were probably no more than fifty people living on the property. The socialist government and non-extradition policy of Guyana were the main attractions for Jones to come there. In 1977, the Guyanaese government cautiously granted the Peoples Temple permission to start building their utopian complex, which was met with warm welcomes. If Jones could be isolated from society, he could finally achieve his longtime goal of establishing a Marxist society. What transpired, however, was darker and more dangerous than anybody had anticipated. Jones would spend his nights lecturing fervently on the ills of society and critiquing defectors harshly. Concurrently, there were a lot of 10-hour shifts throughout the day.

Cinema nights were no longer filled with enjoyable amusement, but with Soviet-style documentaries depicting the perils, excesses, and vices of the outside world. Due of their restricted skills, the Peoples Temple could only communicate with the outside world through shortwave radios. Inadequate resources were exacerbated by the facility's location on barren terrain. Stories of cult members being beaten, confined in small cages shaped like coffins, and even forced to sleep in dry wells circulated across Guyana. It started to alarm a lot of people that Jones was losing touch with reality. To try to stop his illness from becoming worse, he began taking amphetamines and pentobarbital in potentially fatal doses. As he announced that the US had descended into chaos, his more somber and muddled speech, which was carried via the multiple speakers almost continuously, became increasingly unsettling. The turning point came, however, when Jones found out that an exposé describing his conduct was going to be released. Discussions with members who have passed on were highlighted in the piece. Hundreds of Peoples Temple adherents, including Jim Jones, arrived in Guyana just before the report was intended to be published. They settled down inside the Jonestown compound. The year 1974 saw a pilgrimage of the most dedicated Jones supporters to the South American country of Guyana. A communal farm was to be established in the middle of the jungle. Guyana is unique among South American nations in having English as its official language since it gained independence from the UK in 1966. In 1977, Jones moved to Guyana with more than a thousand other members of the Temple. The utopia their leader had promised was not to be found in Jonestown, alas. The members of the temple worked long hours in the fields and faced harsh punishments if they dared to question Jones' authority. The authorities confiscated their passports and any medication they possessed, while tropical diseases and mosquitoes were at an epidemic level. Just beyond the jungle compound stood a small group of armed soldiers. Participants were required to meet first thing in the morning on a regular basis and were strongly encouraged to update each other. Their emails and phone conversations were filtered and listened to. While at the peak of his authority, Jones compared himself to people from history, such as Vladimir Lenin and Jesus Christ. Actually, he had his personal throne set up in the main pavilion of the estate. The government, the media, and his detractors were all involved in his demise, in his mind. "Suicide drills," in which Peoples Temple members were compelled to jump out of windows, also took place at midnight.

CHAPTER THREE

Jonestown: The Brutal Truth

The driving force behind Jonestown was the creation of a perfect society. The promises made to them were not kept at Jonestown. To maximize the limited space during construction, the cottages were equipped with bunk beds. Due to the rigid gender separation in the cabins, even married couples had to be apart. The intense heat and humidity in Jonestown made many people sick. Additionally, members had to put in 11-hour days regardless of the conditions.

Jones's voice echoed through the speaker system, filling the entire building. It's really annoying that Jones keeps talking on the loudspeaker late into the night. They attempted to catch some sleep after working hard on their tasks. Some Jonestowners were satisfied with their lives as they were, while others longed for the chance to escape. Before anyone could leave the facility, they all had to get Jones's approval. The compound, nestled deep within the jungle, was guarded by armed soldiers. Jones stated that everyone had to remain.

A Heart-breaking End for Leo Ryan

Jonestown was running smoothly until Leo Ryan arrived and disrupted everything. Ryan and other US representatives were captivated by the distorted body of a cult member at the Peoples Temple. For two years before, Ryan and this cult member had been friends. A group of eighteen people, among them a few journalists, set off for Guyana five days before the Jonestown Massacre, with Ryan at the helm. Their journey aimed to connect with Jones and his supporters. After receiving reports from worried citizens about the unjust imprisonment of family members in Jonestown, California, Congressman Leo Ryan chose to visit the area to see for himself. In November 1978, Ryan led a group to Guyana. Photographers, reporters, and worried family members of Peoples Temple members all contributed to this gathering. On November 17th, the Jonestown compound planned to host a surprise dinner and an evening of entertainment for the congressman and the media present. Jones became even more willing when it came to doing interviews. During their time in Jonestown, several members of the Peoples Temple pleaded with Ryan's group for assistance in escaping. Initially, Ryan and his team thought they had everything managed. While the other guests savored a delicious meal and danced the night away, a quiet group of individuals discreetly shared their intentions with an NBC crew member. Afterward, evidence surfaced showing that several Jonestowners were coerced into captivity. Ryan didn't have to stress over a poor settlement. Ryan noticed that many of the cultists seemed to have chosen to be part of the organization, even though they were living in terrible conditions. After surveying the group of more than 600 adults, Ryan determined that the departure of twelve should not be a cause for concern. Even though some of his companions had shown interest in going too, this remained true. On the other hand, Jim Jones felt completely defeated. Even though Ryan kept insisting that the Peoples Temple would clear the inspection, Jones was sure that Ryan would alert the right authorities since he planned to get them involved. On November 18, 1978, the next day, Ryan announced that he would offer transportation to anyone wanting to go back to the United States. Ryan made an offer, but only a handful of people took it up because they were worried about how Jones would react. When it became clear that it was time to leave, the members of the Peoples Temple who had previously expressed their wish to leave Jonestown quickly got into a vehicle with Ryan and his companions.

A member of the Peoples Temple assaulted Ryan, who remained behind to ensure that no one else was trying to escape, before the car had traveled very far. Ryan and his friends found themselves in serious peril as the assailant closed in, the threat looming over them. Once he left the building, Ryan hopped into the pickup. Although the planes were not ready for takeoff when the truck got to the airport, everything else was in order. They were waiting at a nearby jungle airstrip when they were attacked by Jim

Jones's mercenaries. While they were still waiting, a trailer and truck pulled up. A sneak peek reveals that a group from the Peoples Temple suddenly appeared and launched an attack on Ryan and his friends. Sadly, a photographer for the San Francisco Examiner, a woman from the Peoples Temple trying to escape, and Ryan, a cameraman and reporter for NBC, all lost their lives.

CHAPTER FOUR

Jonestown Tragedy

When they got back to Jonestown, Jones called for a meeting to be held under the pavilion. After the meeting wrapped up, Jones stepped up to deliver the sermon. It seemed as though he was suffering immensely and losing his mind. After the unexpected death of the congressman, the people's temple and Jim Jones faced a significant obstacle to their ongoing existence. Jones painted a picture for his followers of a government that was utterly mad and corrupt, cautioning that the authorities could come "parachuting in" at any time, yet he was caught off guard by his own arrest. He cautioned his followers that doom was approaching and urged them to take their lives without delay. He felt even more betrayed knowing that some of his friends had left him behind. It seemed that time was incredibly important to him. In his speech to the assembly, he warned of a potential attack on Ryan's gang. He told them that Jonestown was no longer safe after the attack. Jones suggested that the US government might respond forcefully after the attack on Ryan's group. Jones has voiced his worry that someone might start parachuting in and firing from above, endangering the lives of helpless infants. In

Jones's perspective, suicide is seen as a "revolutionary act" that could enhance the lives of those who follow him. Once Jones explained why all other options were pointless, the crowd swiftly shifted their focus to a woman who had voiced her opposition to the proposal. In the audio recording, the adults reassure the children that their cries aren't because of any physical discomfort, but instead because of the somewhat bitter flavour of the pills. Evidence on the substance indicates that the drugs were likely given by squirting them into the mouth. A number of people feel a strong sense of duty to Jones, as they think they wouldn't have survived without his help. As long as it leads to settling the score with him, they're ready to risk everything for it. After taking the poison, some onlookers might question why those who are dying don't appear to be happier. When a parent understands that their child is safe and out of harm's way from the enemy, a sense of gratitude washes over them. Jones spoke up passionately, encouraging everyone to start moving. Outside the pavilion, there were large kettles filled with Valium and grape-flavored Flavor-Aid laced with cyanide. The toxic liquid was injected into them with syringes. The mothers were the ones who ultimately lost their lives as a result. They kept going in the same way. It took a while for the rest of the group to get their drinks since quite a few of them were no longer around. If anyone put up a fight, there were guards ready with crossbows and guns. The average time until death was five minutes.

A Documentary on the Victims of Death

On November 18, 1978, a harmful chemical led to the deaths of approximately 912 people, including 276 children. It's uncertain if Jones shot himself in the head on purpose, but he was discovered dead from the injury. Many individuals struggled significantly to leave the enclosure or venture into the wilderness. Officials from Guyana arrived the next day, preparing for armed individuals, security personnel, and an angry Jim Jones at the entrance. If there was any resistance, they were prepared. They got there to find a peaceful scene. The remains of many victims were discovered entwined in what seemed to be a final embrace. A 47-year-old man named Jim Jones was discovered sitting in a chair with a gunshot wound to the head, suggesting that he ended his own life. On that day, in another area of Guyana, several members of the Peoples Temple were present, including a few of Jones' sons. Meanwhile, a few others managed to enter the woodland without any issues. There are theories suggesting that the poisoners might have acted as if they were merely conducting a dry run, with the intention of ensuring no one would be harmed. The "death tape," which recorded the chilling audio of the incident, served as a crucial resource for the police in their efforts to piece together the events that unfolded earlier. More than a thousand audio recordings revealed the propaganda, group discussions, and sermons of the Peoples Temple. The shocking techniques employed by the group came to light in these recordings. Members of the Guyana Temple who managed to escape the massacre either left on the same day or were in Georgetown, the capital, at the time of the incident. There were fewer than a hundred of them. The authorities later found a wide array of weapons, passports, and half a million dollars in cash. They also found that accounts in different countries have received millions of dollars. After the disaster, the Peoples Temple declared bankruptcy in late 1978. In the United States, Larry Layton, a member of the Temple, was the sole individual held responsible for the events of November 18th. In 2002, his life sentence was reduced even though he was involved in the conspiracy, which involved helping with Ryan's murder and the attempted murder of

Richard Dwyer, a U.S. embassy officer. The Guyanan government has sentenced Charles Beikman to five years in prison for the attempted murder of a girl. Eighty members of the Peoples Temple managed to survive the ordeal in Guyana. A large crowd showed up from Southern California and the San Francisco Bay Area too. Once everything calms down, this heartbreaking incident will likely be labeled as a "mass suicide." Expressions such as "they drank the Kool-Aid" indicate that this phenomenon remains significant in today's context. Your belief that everyone has "drank the Kool-Aid" is entirely baseless. Unfortunately, not all the casualties that day were by choice. A significant number of people, including kids and seniors, were forcibly administered cyanide injections.

Lessons from Jonestown

Jonestown stands out as one of the most tragic cult-related massacres in history, claiming the lives of over 900 unsuspecting individuals. While we can't change what has happened, we can take away important lessons from this tragedy to help protect us from future horrors: It's important to approach ideologies that require blind loyalty or rely on charismatic leaders with a critical and skeptical mindset. Encourage others to question influential figures and to confront extreme or manipulative perspectives.

Encourage Open Conversations: Foster a space that appreciates and promotes open conversation. Encourage an open environment where people can ask questions and share their concerns about sensitive topics without worrying about being judged. A person in need of your protection may be someone who feels alone in society, faces financial challenges, or is struggling with mental health concerns. Assist them in steering clear of exploitation by offering resources and connections they can rely on. Improving mental health services and early intervention programs is essential to ensure that mental health issues are tackled quickly as they arise. Helping and supporting people with mental health challenges could protect them from manipulative leaders. Increase understanding of cult behaviors and the methods employed by manipulative leaders to influence their followers. It's important for the community to understand the signs of cult members and how to support those who may be at risk. Embrace a leadership approach that prioritizes honesty, accountability, and receptiveness to ideas. Being an effective leader means being receptive to feedback and acknowledging your mistakes when they happen. Help prevent people from being misled and put at risk by clarifying their misunderstandings. Promote the growth of analytical thinking skills, encompassing proficiency in different forms of media. Highlight the Importance of Distinct Viewpoints We should support independent thinking and seek out information from a range of sources. When trying to understand complicated matters, it's important to maintain a balanced viewpoint and steer clear of extremes. Design an environment that allows everyone to unwind and have a good time. Create an environment that honors the fundamental worth and freedom of each person. Friendship and community networks can provide individuals at risk of joining dangerous groups with a renewed sense of belonging and safety by enhancing their existing support systems. The lessons society has learned from the Jonestown Massacre might aid in preventing future atrocities. It's essential to stay alert and dedicated to creating a community that values reason, compassion, and safeguarding those who are most at risk from harm and deception.

END

Printed in Dunstable, United Kingdom